FUNDAMENTALISM

Fundamentalism

A Pastoral Concern

Eugene LaVerdiere, S.S.S.

A Liturgical Press Book

THE LITURGICAL PRESS
Collegeville, Minnesota

Cover design by David Manahan, O.S.B.

1 2 3 4 5 6 7 8

Library of Congress Cataloging-in-Publication Data

LaVerdiere, Eugene.
Fundamentalism : a pastoral concern / Eugene LaVerdiere.
p. cm.
Includes bibliographical references.
ISBN 0-8146-2713-7 (alk. paper)
1. Fundamentalism. I. Title.
BT82.2.L39 2000
230'.04626—dc21 99-39498
CIP

If importance is to be measured by influence, fundamentalism is one of the most important movements in Christianity today. We can trace its roots to the Reformation with its emphasis on *sola scriptura*, to the modern Western world with its spirit of individualism, and to the evangelical spirit of Christian evangelicalism.

It emerged as a recognizable phenomenon at the end of the nineteenth century with a series of conferences in New York, Chicago, and Niagara. The participants came from various denominations, but they had a common concern that the traditional faith was being eroded in their Churches as well as in public life and in public education.

At the beginning of the twentieth century, between 1910 and 1915, a group of Protestant theologians, preachers, and evangelists articulated their stance in a series of tracts entitled *The Fundamentals, a Testimony to the Truth*. From the beginning these tracts echoed the beliefs and feelings of many, not only in the United States but also in many other parts of the English-speaking world.

Comprising twelve volumes, *The Fundamentals* have become the *magna carta* of fundamentalism, at least in its more thoughtful Christian expression. Today, the basic positions of most fundamentalist preachers remain essentially the same as those set forth in *The Fundamentals*. For the most part the tracts in *The Fundamentals* can be classed as a work of apologetics, defending the basics. The twelve volumes also include personal testimony, tracts on evangelism, Bible study, and polemic tracts against the enemies of fundamentalism, including "Mormonism" (Latter Day Saints), "Eddyism" (Christian Science), but especially "Romanism" (the Roman Catholic Church).

Fundamentalism has long been associated with a number of Protestant Churches, some of which are quite small and fairly obscure, but others are extremely large with highly developed skills at mass communication. The larger

Churches have an enormous following outside of their own membership. They also influence the religious attitudes of Christians belonging to main-line Churches. As ministers of the word, we are repeatedly asked to respond to the issues and the problems they raise.

In recent years fundamentalism has been making significant inroads in the Roman Catholic Church, not only in the United States but also especially in Latin America and the Philippines. Not that we have ever been altogether free of it. Never before, however, have we experienced it in its present form, where Catholics personally opt for a fundamentalist stance toward Scripture and its bearing on Christian life. A committed fundamentalism, as opposed to unconscious fundamental influence, is new for us. Having little experience with it, many do not know how to respond.

A Descriptive Definition

For many people, fundamentalism hardly needs defining. They know it from the preaching of fundamentalist evangelists on television. They also associate it with the various fundamentalist interpretations of the days of creation, which some fundamentalists accept as taking place literally on the six days that preceded the first Sabbath. Other fundamentalists interpret the six days as six consecutive eras, beginning with the first, when God created light, and climaxing with the creation of humankind. To understand the nature of fundamentalism, however, it is very helpful to have a descriptive definition.

The word "fundamentalist" was coined by Curtis Lee Laws and first used in print in an editorial in the July 1, 1920 issue of *The Watchman-Examiner*, a Baptist paper published in New York. The editorial witnesses to the spirit of early fundamentalism.

> We here and now move that a new word be adopted to describe the men among us who insist that the landmarks shall

> not be removed. "Conservatives" is too closely allied with reactionary forces in all walks of life. "Premillennialists" is too closely allied with a single doctrine and not sufficiently inclusive. "Landmarkers" has a historical disadvantage and connotes a particular group of radical conservatives. We suggest that those who still cling to the great fundamentals and who mean to do battle royal for the fundamentals shall be called "Fundamentalists." By that name the editor of *The Watchman-Examiner* is willing to be called. It will be understood therefore when he uses the word it will be in compliment and not in disparagement.

George Marsden, a professor of history at Calvin College in Grand Rapids, Michigan, provided a helpful definition in an article entitled "Fundamentalism as an American Phenomenon: A Comparison with English Evangelicalism":

> A twentieth-century movement closely tied to the revivalist tradition of mainstream evangelical Protestantism that militantly opposed modernist theology and the cultural change associated with it.
>
> *Church History,* 46/2 (June 1977) 215

Marsden's definition was welcomed by Ed Dobson, Ed Hindson, and Jerry Falwell in their *The Fundamentalist Phenomenon*. In this book these authors also described fundamentalism as a "reaffirmation of evangelical Christianity" and "reactionary Evangelicalism" (p. 3). They also presented fundamentalism as a non-conformist movement directed against the impact of Darwinism, higher biblical criticism, and liberal theology, all of which they saw as nothing but a new form or rationalism and secularism (p. 4).

We can also describe fundamentalism as a reactionary, ideological movement in evangelical Protestantism.

• As a movement, its goal is to preserve the basics of the Christian faith, particularly the literal teaching in the Bible.

• As a reactionary movement, its goal is to snuff out modernism, liberalism, and secular humanism in their Churches.

• As an ideological movement, it tends to simplify the problems facing Christianity. As such, it has simple objectives and simple solutions. Like every ideology, fundamentalists tend to focus on one or two enemies and to use slogans to describe them.

• As a Protestant movement, its goal is to reform the Church. They take the Reformation very seriously, and they oppose the ecumenical movement. ?

• As a movement in evangelical Protestantism, its goal to revive the militant spirit of the Reformation and to purify and renew Christianity with the teaching of the Bible.

Fundamentalism began as a reaction to modernism, liberalism, or secular humanism. As such, fundamentalism was a response to a real problem, but it itself turned out to be a real problem. Its foundations were two narrow and, paradoxically, not very evangelical. For us, fundamentalism is a big challenge. We can divide the problem or challenge of fundamentalism in five areas. For Roman Catholics and main-line Churches, it is a theological challenge as well as a pastoral challenge. It is also a social challenge and a personal challenge. Especially, fundamentalism is an evangelical challenge.

A Theological Challenge

Fundamentalism is a theological challenge. To understand the theological nature of Christian fundamentalism and to situate its challenge, it is important first to describe it theologically.

First, it should be pointed out that for fundamentalists the biblical word is seen as an absolute, as a reality in itself whose statement is clear and unchanging. It is not relative to the understanding of those who hear it in varying cultural and historical contexts. As a result, it does not require interpretation. In a sense fundamentalism is not a kind of interpretation but a denial of the need and legitimacy of interpretation. It presupposes that the word can be immediately grasped by all.

Unwittingly, however, the fundamentalist does interpret. Such is the nature of reading and communication. Everyone reads the Bible through the lens of their experience, cultural and personal. Without realizing it the fundamentalist equates the biblical word with his or her interpretation of it and presents their interpretation as absolute, as the one interpretation for all that hear the word. Hence the frustration of anyone who tries to discuss the meaning of a verse of Scripture with a fundamentalist. The very ground for discussion is denied from the start, and no progress can be made.

Second, the fundamentalist views the biblical word as the absolute point of departure for knowing the truth in faith. The Scriptures, however, both in their origins and in their traditional role in the Church, presuppose a life experience of God and faith. Life and faith come first. For the Israelites and the early Christians, the Scriptures formulated life and faith and inspired those who share them to grow religiously as they faced history's challenges. The same has been true in the Church's tradition, and this is how the Church presents the Scriptures today. For the fundamentalist, the biblical word comes first. Life and faith follow. This approach leaves little or no room for development in revelation. For fundamentalists the scriptural word does not represent a quest for understanding in which faith reaches for God and progressively opens itself to revelation.

Third, a fundamentalist stance views the biblical word as a divine word, which it is. It also stresses the divinity of Jesus as the Son of God. In doing so, however, it practically denies the humanity of the word and has no emphasis on Jesus' humanity. Like Jesus, the biblical word is both fully human and fully divine. The Second Vatican Council compared the scriptural word to the humanity and divinity of Jesus:

> Indeed the words of God, expressed in the words of men, are in every way like human language, just as the Word of the eternal Father, when he took on himself the flesh of human weakness, became like men.
>
> *Dogmatic Constitution on Divine Revelation,* #13

The biblical word is spoken in a particular language with a genius and mode of communication special to it. People who speak more than one language know that every language is unique. Biblical writing also reflects a certain world-view as well as the faith, human sensitivity, and literary style of its authors. For example, there is a vast difference between the book of Isaiah and the book of Proverbs. Anyone can sense the difference between Paul's letters and the gospel narratives.

The Church accounts for these differences by viewing the scriptural word as a divine word, which is expressed in human words, and also as a human word, which speaks the divine word. The Scriptures are consequently like the person of Jesus in whom the word that was in the beginning, the word that was with God, indeed, the word that was God (see John 1:1) "became flesh and made his dwelling among us" (see John 1:14). Jesus is "the only Son, God, who is at the Father's side, has revealed him" in his incarnation (see John 1:18).

Failure to appreciate the humanity of the divine word sometimes has terrible consequences, as we see today in some parts of the Moslem world, which also has its fundamentalists. When human beings act on a word that they judge to be purely divine, they may engage in actions which common sense and decency label as inhuman. With a lopsided view of the divinity of the word, we can easily think of ourselves as divine, and our divine word becomes an inhuman word.

Fourth, fundamentalist interpretation is often associated with an apocalyptic view of history. This is so often the case that fundamentalism and apocalyptic attitudes are almost inseparable in the mind of many. Contemporary apocalyptic attitude finds little or no hope in the created world. So permeated by evil, the world is not redeemable. It consequently focuses sharply on the cataclysmic end of the world in divine judgment.

In its association with apocalyptic attitudes, fundamentalism fails to recognize the goodness of God's creation. With no emphasis on the incarnation and the humanity of the divine word in Scripture, it has little place for sacraments, which presuppose that human beings and earthly realities, like the human word, can express and communicate divine realities. To do this, the earthly realities have to be seen as good.

Fundamentalism, however, can also be allied with politics and economics. In this case, it usually reinforces the political and economic *status quo* with divine warrant. Theologically, it does away with the grounds for separating Church and State in a pluralist society and works to impose its views on everyone. In both its political and apocalyptic associations, fundamentalism has been often welcomed and supported by repressive governments, which recognize that its religious stance is rarely a threat to them.

A Pastoral Challenge

From the above considerations on the theological implications of fundamentalism, it should be obvious that fundamentalism is primarily a pastoral problem, not only a problem of biblical interpretation. By engaging fundamentalists on their own ground, we too easily slip into fundamentalism ourselves. We might outwit a fundamentalist in public debate, but our position on the Scriptures would then have little value beyond the *ad hominem* argument that supports it. It would do little to nourish the Christian community.

Rather, the question to ask is why fundamentalists need to assume a fundamentalist stance toward the Scriptures. Why do fundamentalists need absolutes and absolute certitude? Why do they find it necessary to emphasize the priority of the Scriptures over life and faith? Why do they cling to the divinity of the word at the expense of its human expression? And whence come the popular alliances between fundamentalism and contemporary apocalyptic tendencies and political and economic power?

These questions indicate that we would do better with a pastoral approach to fundamentalists rather than a biblical approach. Fundamentalism is but a symptom of broad socio-religious and personal problems that Christians cannot dismiss and against which arguments are futile. The symptom will not disappear unless we apply a pastoral remedy to its root causes. At best, it will reappear in a new form, as when someone abandons faith and substitutes secular absolutes for religious absolutes. In winning a biblical argument, we might well lose a Christian.

The most basic question is whether fundamentalists require our pastoral attention as much as those who are not fundamentalist or who have no interest in the Scriptures. Fundamentalists are persons. They have deep human needs like the rest of us. God loves them and calls them to salvation. Must we not respond to their needs and reach out to them with the Lord's loving mercy?

A Social Challenge

It would be very nearsighted to treat fundamentalism as a purely personal problem. Its vast popular appeal should alert us to this. Fundamentalism is a social problem, and so we should respond to its challenge with the same breadth of vision that we bring to other social challenges.

First, the fact that modern fundamentalism reaches across church boundaries and even cuts across the world's major religions indicates that it springs from the social instability, cultural transformations, demographic dislocations, and sweeping changes which are so obvious in the modern world. In the face of these, a large segment of the human population is bound to suffer from enormous insecurity.

Unable to cope with such instability, many turn to the absolute authority of a divine Word that they grasp in a fundamentalist way. Fundamentalism tries to cling to the literal sense, but without attending to the literary context, to the nature of the word, and what the word evokes, they stray from the literal sense. The literal meaning of a symbol or a metaphor is symbolic or metaphorical. An image should not be reduced to a flat statement. The literal meaning is extremely important. Without it, we cannot understand and appreciate the biblical word. With the Pontifical Biblical Commission, what the fundamentalists call "literal" we call a "literalist" interpretation:

> Fundamentalist interpretation starts from the principle that the Bible, being the Word of God, inspired and free from error, should be read and interpreted literally in all its details. But by "literal interpretation" it understands a naively literalist interpretation, one, that is to say, which excludes every effort at understanding the Bible that takes account of its historical origins and development.
>
> *The Interpretation of the Bible in the Church* (I. F)

We could add that the fundamentalist interpretation does not take account of the literary nature of the Scriptures.

Second, we note that fundamentalism is most rampant among the poor, in depressed areas, and among those who have seen nearly every fact of life change and who find themselves struggling to find a stable footing in life. It should not surprise us to find fundamentalists in populations of poor immigrants for whom Church structures in the land to which they have immigrated are inadequate. Nor should it amaze us to find it among those who find themselves suddenly out of work and who watch their savings daily erode.

We should also expect to find fundamentalism among students who struggle with their studies and who know that even if they succeed they may not find a place for themselves in the world of work. Should we wonder that such people see the world around them as coming to an end? Even among the wealthy and middle class, fundamentalism can provide a buttress against changes that threaten their way of life, privilege, and status.

Third, committed Roman Catholic fundamentalism among those who had once been "ordinary" Catholics requires special consideration. Such fundamentalism may be related directly to changes in the way Church authority is viewed, assumed, and exercised. It is not so long ago that the spoken word of a person in authority in the Church was accepted without question. Should we not view this response as a fundamentalism of the spoken word, a word spoken by one that enjoyed God's authority and commanded absolute and uncritical obedience? Rightful changes in the exercise of authority in the Church and the unfortunate erosion of legitimate authority have undermined the security that this authority once provided.

The need for absolutes, however, did not disappear with these changes. Deeply felt, it simply redirected its attention to the written word of the Bible. In a sense, then, we have long had a fundamentalist streak within the Church. The thing that has changed is that we now have a fundamentalism of the written word rather of the spoken word. The new stance is bound to be difficult for anyone in authority and for a Church which values the personal presence of God in the world above every verbal articulation of that presence.

Another difference between the two manifestations of fundamentalism lies in the fact that the spoken word allowed for considerable development. It could change, and its exaggerations could be balanced or be tempered by the spoken word of another person in authority. It left room for appeal. The written word, however, is fixed and inflexible. The fundamentalism associated with it, consequently, is apt to be far more radical and even more despotic than that of the spoken word.

When human ills stem from a social situation, we cannot expect to deal with them adequately on a personal and individualized basis. There are no simple answers. As a complex social problem, fundamentalism calls for a multifaceted social response. From this perspective, the pastoral task appears far greater than we probably had anticipated.

For people who find themselves rootless and isolated in an inhospitable world, we must try to provide small communities in which people find needed support and basic security. The fight against fundamentalism is also a fight against poverty and human degradation. It calls for the kind of evangelization that enables people to see their worth as God's creatures, for which Christ gave his life. That evangelization should lead to genuine concern for others. As these objectives are met, there is no *raison d'etre* for fundamentalism.

A Personal Challenge

Although fundamentalism is a social challenge, we usually meet it as a personal challenge. Fundamentalism is a personal problem both for fundamentalists and those who come in contact with them.

Fundamentalists themselves do not view their fundamentalism as a problem. They see it as a solution to a problem or to many problems. Unfortunately, it is not an adequate solution. The Scriptures should help us to deal effectively with basic life issues. They should enable us to transform our environment, to find our Christian way in life, and to contribute to the betterment of others. With a fundamentalist interpretation, however, they provide an easy escape that reinforces dropout tendencies. Responding to this personal problem, we must help fundamentalists to face and accept their situation in life as a point of departure for personal transformation. This is better done indirectly, by providing loving support, than by directly taking on the fundamentalist on biblical grounds.

Fundamentalism is also a personal problem for anyone who cares about the life of the Church and who has accepted a pastoral responsibility in it. It is a problem first because we love the Scriptures as well as the people we serve, including fundamentalists, and because we find ourselves so helpless when confronted by a fundamentalist.

The Scriptures belong to all of us. Like the fundamentalist, we too appropriate the Scriptures and find life through them. Outwardly, both the fundamentalist and the non-fundamentalist stand on the same ground, that is, the Scriptures. However, denied the right to interpret the Scriptures, we find ourselves deprived of one of our most basic resources for articulating and orienting Christian life. Since in their security, fundamentalists find it necessary to impose their interpretation on everyone else, they also threaten our entire pastoral effort.

The only viable response to this twofold personal problem lies in our gradual purification as ministers of the word. Insecurity, rigidity, and illusory power cannot be met by the same behavior. The temptation to raise our voices or to ridicule is strong. Our best response to fundamentalism, indeed the only genuinely Christian response, consists in a pastoral concern for which we have such a fine example in the life and work of Jesus. The answer to fundamentalism is not a biblical argument but the strength of faith and the power of love, the dual wellspring of hope and the true Christian security.

An Evangelical Challenge

After everything is said and done, however, the fundamentalists have a point. Surely there must be something so basic, so fundamental, that if we deny or abandon it we are not Christians anymore. It is the same for Catholics. Surely there must be something so basic that if a Catholic denies it, he or she is not Catholic anymore. The question is to identify the fundamentals.

Fundamentalists agree on five fundamentals:

1) the inspiration and inerrancy of the Bible,
2) the divinity and virgin birth of Christ,
3) the substitutionary atonement of Christ's death,
4) the literal bodily resurrection of Christ from the dead, and
5) the literal return of Christ in the second coming.

Suppose Catholics were to draw up a list of fundamentals, I wonder what we would include in our list. Would it vary from one part of the Church to the next? Would a list drawn up in Nairobi be the same as one from New York? Would a list from the sixteenth century be the same as one from the twentieth? Would it include the work of the Holy Spirit, collegiality in the Church's leadership, the existence of angels, the primacy of Peter, bringing good news to the poor? Would Lutherans not want to include justification by faith?

Asking such questions helps us to appreciate what it means to establish and affirm a number of fundamentals. But it also leads us to ask why we should want to do this. Is it that we need criteria to test orthodoxy? Are we looking for the truths that witness to our unity as Catholics coming from different cultural and social backgrounds? Or is it that we want to profess our faith in a manner that announces our identity as Christians and Catholics? The biggest challenge is to be evangelical. Our fundamentals should be an expression of our evangelical spirit.

If our Christian and Catholic identity is the fundamental issue, why would we want to establish a list of abstractions or truths like the existence of God, creation, redemption, and the nature of grace? Rather, should we not turn to divine mysteries, things hidden in God which are gradually revealed in historical events and which envelop us in God's life? Such is the stuff of our traditional creeds.

Fundamentals have always been part of the life of the Church. But we do not call them fundamentals. We call them creeds. Like the fundamentalists' list of fundamentals, a creed is a simple summary of the basic Christian beliefs, but it is a very special kind of summary.

The creed is in the form of a story, and it includes a whole series of events. We have an excellent example of such a creed in 1 Corinthians 15:3-5:

> Christ died for our sins in accordance with the scriptures; . . . he was buried; . . . he was raised on the third day in accordance with the scriptures; . . . he appeared to Kephas, then to the Twelve.

The creed includes four events; Christ died, he was buried, he rose, and he appeared. Christianity is a historical religion, and its fundamentals consequently must be historical. In our creed we stand in wonder before the great events in which Christ's life culminated. The fundamental beliefs in our creed are not primarily abstract truths to be analyzed but events to be contemplated and be witnessed to.

For the early Christians of Antioch, where this creed was handed on to Paul, and for the Christians in Corinth, who received it from him, the four events given in 1 Corinthians 15:3-5 constituted the basics, the fundamentals. It does not mean that nothing else was important. But in their time and circumstances, other things could be presumed. Like prayers, creeds are expandable according to the pastoral, cultural, and social needs. The fundamental events in the creed are fleshed out in the Gospels in the New Testament.

Unlike the five fundamentals, the basic events in the creed are not a purely objective set of beliefs independent of the experience of the believers. The events in the creed involve us: "Christ died for *our* sins." The events told in the creed are not part of someone else's story. They tell our story. We live in the same history that was marked and transformed by the death, burial and resurrection of Jesus Christ. Like Paul, we have to pass on the fundamentals that we received. We have to pass on our story. Doing that, we will respond to the challenges of fundamentalism.

Recommended Readings on Fundamentalism

Barr, James. *Beyond Fundamentalism*. Philadelphia: The Westminster Press, 1984.

____. *Fundamentalism*. Philadelphia: The Westminster Press, 1978.

Bergant, Dianne, C.S.A. "Fundamentalism and the Biblical Commission." *Chicago Studies* 34/3 (December 1995) 209–21.

Cohen, Norman J., ed. *The Fundamentalist Phenomenon: A View from Within; a Response from Without*. Grand Rapids, Mich.: W. B. Eerdmans, 1991.

Dobson, Ed, Ed Hinsom, and Jerry Falwell. *The Fundamentalist Phenomenon*, 2nd Edition. Grand Rapids, Mich.: Baker Book House, 1986.

Hoppe, Leslie J., O.F.M. "Premillenial Dispensationalism: Fundamentalism's Eschatological Scenario." *Chicago Studies* 34/3 (December 1995) 222–35.

Kung, Hans, and Jurgen Moltmann, eds. *Fundamentalism as an Ecumenical Challenge* (Concilium 1992/3) London: SCM Press, 1992.

Marsden, George M. *Fundamentalism and American Culture: The Shaping of Twentieth-Century Evangelicalism: 1870–1925*. New York: Oxford University Press, 1980.

____. "Fundamentalism as an American Phenomenon: A Comparison with English Evangelicalism." *Church History* 46/2 (June 1977) 215–32.

____. *Understanding Fundamentalism and Evangelicalism*. Grand Rapids, Mich.: W. B. Eerdmans, 1991.

Marty, Martin E., and R. Scott Appleby. *The Fundamentalisms Project.* Chicago: University of Chicago Press. 5 vols.
Vol. 1 *Fundamentalisms Observed.* 1991.
Vol. 2 *Fundamentalisms and Society: Reclaiming the Sciences, the Family, and Education.* 1993.
Vol. 3 *Fundamentalisms and the State: Remaking Politics, Economics, And Militance.* 1993.
Vol. 4 *Accounting for Fundamentalisms: The Dynamic Character of Movements.* 1994.
Vol. 5 *Fundamentalisms Comprehended.* 1995.
Norris, Frederick W. *The Apostolic Faith: Protestants and Roman Catholics.* Collegeville: The Liturgical Press, 1992.
O'Meara, Thomas F., O.P. *Fundamentalism: A Catholic Perspective.* New York: Paulist Press, 1990.
The Pontifical Biblical Commission. *The Interpretation of the Bible in the Church.* Vatican City: Libreria Editrice Vaticana, 1993.